£10

$9.95

the wacky world of SKIING

by Craig Peterson

Cartoons by
Jerry Emerson

First Printing

ISBN 0-913276-31-6   Library of Congress Card No. 80-52424

Jacket design by Kathy Jungjohann.

Text layout by Pamela Haran.

STONE WALL PRESS, INC.
1241 30th Street, N.W.
Washington, D.C. 20007

Ph: (202) 333-1860

Distributed by

THE STEPHEN GREENE PRESS, INC.
Box 1000
Brattleboro, Vt. 05301

the wacky world of SKIING

JERRY EMERSON is a self-taught freelance cartoonist from Massachusetts. His cartoons have appeared in major magazines, trade journals, and medical and scientific periodicals. Specifically, some of these magazines include: *Saturday Evening Post*, *New Woman*, *Saturday Review*, *Omni*, *Parade* and *Reader's Digest.* All of the cartoons appearing here are original and have been prepared especially for this book.

CRAIG PETERSON

For the past six years I have been a gagwriter for the top cartoonists in the field. My work has been published in hundreds of magazines, books, and newspapers, both in the United States and abroad. I am also a skier—downhill and cross-country. In addition, I've worked in the ski business for three years, first as a ski technician and later as a shop manager. Due to this experience, I believe I know cartoons, skiing and, more importantly, skiers themselves—what they identify with and what they might find amusing.

There are many fine ski books available on technique, vacations, etc., but to the best of my knowledge there is no cartoon book dealing with skiing. My collection is unique in that it includes humorous cartoon interpretations of actual ski safety tips and cross-country survival tips.

Craig Peterson
Minneapolis, Minnesota
November, 1979

"My ski instructor doesn't understand me."

"You lack self-confidence, Miriam—that shows good sense!"

"Basically, my strategy will be to try and make the other racers helpless with laughter."

"Don't pay any attention to me—I'm still learning!"

"We came to _ski_—remember?!"

"It's more than I ever dared hope for!"

Cross Country Survival Tip #7

When touring the back country, remember the natural environment offers many sources of nutrition for the resourceful.

"Make like you're Jean-Claude Killy."

STANDING

RIDING

Step #3

SKIING

"No, Missy. Jack and Jill didn't use the chairlift to get up the hill."

"No, we don't happen to have an opening for a ski bum."

"Al, do you believe in omens?"

SKIING IN ALASKA

"Now what?"

Ski Safety Tip #33
Do not move an injured skier.

"To tell you the truth, it's the only stunt he knows."

GREAT MOMENTS IN SKIING

With the advanced technology of snow making, skiing is now possible in Egypt.

"Don't move—I want to forget you exactly as you are."

"Hello, Guiness Book of World Records...?"

Cross Country Survival Tip# 11
If a skier becomes extremely tired or exhausted on the trail, he should find a comfortable place to rest.

"Just teach me how to ski—
I already know how to wrestle."

"When the newness wears off, can you store them in the basement?"

"Here comes a troublemaker."

"Watch out for _moguls!_"

"Remember, Charlie—
our marriage counselor says _I_ should _lead_ half the time!"

CORRECT   **INCORRECT**

Ski Safety Tip #24

When crossing in front of any skier, always assume his ability to be minimal.

"*Don't blame yourself, Mr. Jensen. I'm probably doing something wrong.*"

"I'm a beginning, advanced, novice, intermediate.

What equipment do you recommend?"

"It's my own plan for safer skiing!"

Ski Safety Tip #30

To reduce risk, always

limber up your muscles before skiing.

"Comfy?"

"The guru's out skiing in Aspen...I'm his guest host."

"Dear, have you seen my iron?"

"No, ma'am—we don't have any skis with airbags."

"Look! Civilization!"

Ski Safety Tip #29
Always be prepared for the unexpected.

"All right, Murray! Who's Gloria?"

"Our skis are in Florida."

"Hi, neighbor—could I borrow a cup of hot wax?"

Cross Country Survival Tip #13
Take special care when crossing fences.

"These books can be __purchased__ you know!"

Cross Country Survival Tip #8
Certain skis should be cooled before going skiing.

"It's really too bad. Before he lost his nerve, he was your complete jumper."

"The kids are just wild about our new winter home."

"My legs are being recalled for a possible steering defect."

Ski Safety Tip #27
Skiers should keep off closed trails and posted areas.

"I'd sell you a ticket to Missoula, ma'am—but none of our lifts go that way!"

"No, Honey—he's not a _ski_ bum. He's a _bum_ bum."

"I'm worried about Junior. His skis came back without him!"

"*Edna! Will you stop humming 'The Impossible Dream' when I'm trying to concentrate!*"

Ski Courtesy Tip #25
Skiers should not stop where they will obstruct a trail, or where they will not be visible
from above.

". . . Thinks the world of his new skis."

"Dave's the living proof of reincarnation. No one could be as clumsy as he is in one lifetime!"

"Now this pair was owned by a little old lady with acrophobia."

"How long did they say we'd be stuck?"

Ski Safety Tip #10
It is better to go out overdressed than underdressed.

"Yes, sir, when they made him, they broke the mold!"

"Could you keep your eyes peeled for a set of lost car keys?"

Ski Safety Tip #21
Before doing anything unpredictable, first glance behind you.

"No, today I want you to teach my friend.
I learned yesterday."

Ski Courtesy Tip #23
When overtaking another skier, a suitable shout is a courteous warning.

"What happened after I waved to all my fans out there in television land?"

"But it looks so easy on television."

"May I make a suggestion?"

"Harold marches to the beat of a different drummer."

"First and foremost, Mr. Philman, you must learn to relax."

"Bear in mind that my ski boots probably weigh thirty pounds."

Cross Country Survival Tip #9
In the event of a sudden storm, seek shelter and conserve energy.

"About these ski brakes—are they drum or disc?"

"Nonsense, Marge—

it's never too windy for skiing."

"What's that? Another new ski gadget?"

"They say he's the most fearless skier on the mountain."

"*Lionel!* You come down here this *instant!!*"

"First, let's master the snowplow—then we'll consider learning aerials."

"I guess we should exchange licenses?"

"Mirror, mirror, on the wall . . . who's the best dressed skier of them all?"

"This may sound silly,

but I'm beginning to miss the noise, crowds, traffic and smog."

"Then it's agreed, doctors...
the ski boot will have to come off."

"I'll bet Ingemar Stenmark doesn't have to fix his own breakfast!"

"If the skiing is so great, how come we can still get reservations?"

"Sure, what kind of favor?"

"Sure beats the hell out of any ski lock!"

"Being of sound mind and body, I spent every cent on wine, women and skiing!"

Outdoor Books About the Great Outdoors from Stone Wall Press, Inc.

MOVIN' ON: *Equipment & Techniques for Winter Hikers* by Harry Roberts.
135 pages, 6″ × 9″, illustrated, paperback, $4.95.

Harry Roberts "... sets down a lot of good, common-sense advice and he does it in an engaging, unpresumptuous style." Furthermore, "Robert's wilderness techniques work. They work well." (*Mountain Gazette*)
"This is a superb book, even if you are just thinking about *maybe* going winter camping." (*Backpacker*)

MOVIN' OUT: *Equipment & Technique for Hikers* by Harry Roberts.
160 pages, 6″ × 9″, illustrated, index, paperback, $5.95.

Harry Roberts, field editor for *Backpacker*, has written what the International Backpackers Assn. calls "an excellent, down-to-earth book on backpacking information." This updated edition includes solid advice on boots, clothing, packs, and sleeping bags, as well as techniques for staying warm, eating well, and learning to be at home in a natural environment.

BACKWOODS ETHICS: *Environmental Concerns for Hikers and Campers* by Laura & Guy Waterman.
192 pages, 6 1/8″ × 9¼″, paperback, $6.95.

"... undeniably important. They argue that hikers and backpackers must protect natural resources and maintain the 'spirit of wildness' of our country's backwoods... they describe a new code of backwoods ethics they feel is necessary to accommodate the increasing number of hikers in the wilds." (*PW*) Positive and up-beat, this book documents progress while appealing to a raised natural consciousness.
"This is a book worth reading by anyone who is interested in backpacking or climbing." (*Backpacker*)

ENJOYING THE ACTIVE LIFE AFTER FIFTY by Ralph Hopp.
192 pages, 6 1/8″ × 9¼″, photographs, paperback, $5.95.

Those who have resigned themselves to an indoor life can find new worlds of fun and fitness with the 20 activities detailed here. Photographs provide inspiration as well as techniques that make these pastimes safer, more enjoyable and easier.
"An intelligent, informal presentation of the attractions to plus-fifties of outdoor activities." (*Kirkus Reviews*)

SKI TOURING IN NEW ENGLAND AND NEW YORK, A Complete Cross-Country Ski Book by Lance Tapley.
192 pages, 6″ × 9″, photographs, illustrations, paperback, $4.95.

Tapley brings out the nature and background of cross-country skiing in this country, with basic advice on equipment and technique. In addition to the fundamentals of the sport he locates ski-touring areas and details facilities, outfitters, inns, food and price ranges.

INTRODUCING YOUR KIDS TO THE OUTDOORS by Joan Dorsey.
128 pages, 6″ × 9″, photographs, paperback, $4.95.

Beginning with a carefully planned day hike, and proceeding to extended trips, canoeing, bicycling and ski touring, Dorsey presents straight-forward advice about outdoor trips with the kids along.
"Reading this book should encourage you to get right at it this year and give your kids a taste of something more than city life. There is no time like now to begin, so spend $4.95 on this book and you'll never regret it, and neither will your children." (*American Farm Tribune*)

Wild Edibles

THE NATURAL WORLD COOKBOOK, *Complete Gourmet Meals from Wild Edibles* by Joe Freitus.
304 pages, 7½ " × 9¼ ", illustrated, index, cloth, $15.00.

At long last we have a complete and comprehensive cookbook of wild, edible foods for the adventuresome gourmet. Both plants (Alpine Bilberry to Wintercress) and animals (fish, fowl and game) are included, along with beautiful line drawings by Salli Haberman.

Fare ranges from the usual (Blueberry and Pecan Pies) to the sublime (False Solomon's Seal Souffle); from the common (Bog Cranberry Bread) to the unique (Woodchuck Pie and Armadillo Stew)—hundreds of recipes for complete meals prepared from abundant wild foods found across North America.

WILD PRESERVES, *Illustrated Recipes for Over 100 Natural Jams and Jellies* by Joe Freitus.
192 pages, 5 ¾ " × 8½ ", paperback, $4.95.

"A clever collection for cooks who enjoy the outdoors." (*Savannah New-Press*)
"Joe Freitus has written the creative canner's bible." (*Conservationist*)
A delightful collection of recipes for preserving wild fruit, *WILD PRESERVES* includes jams, jellies, pickles, preserves, conserves, butters and even wine. Well-known wild fruit such as blueberries and blackberries are covered, and the adventurous epicurean will delight in such delicacies as Irish Moss Jelly, Carrion Flower Spice Jelly, and False Solomon's Seal Jam.

160 EDIBLE PLANTS, *Commonly Found in the United States and Canada* by Joe Freitus.
96 pages, 5 ½ " × 8½ ", illustrated, paperback, $3.50.

A handy reference to 160 of the most commonly found edible wild plants throughout the U.S.A. and Canada. Each plant is listed in alphabetical order and accompanied by a line drawing. Thorough descriptions, including habitat, range, edible properties, and preparation.

For the Fisherman

BACKPACKING FOR TROUT by Bill Cairns.
128 pages, 6″ × 9″, photographs, cloth, $12.95.

As the major trout streams become more crowded and less productive, adventuresome fishermen seek out small streams with better opportunities. In this book you will find practical information and advice on how to make your next fishing trip more successful. Planning the trip, the latest in equipment, appropriate technique, and important tips are all carefully discussed.

BENEATH THE RISING MIST by Dana S. Lamb.
142 pages, 7 3/8″ × 9½″, illustrated, cloth, $15.00.

"Like the best of poems of Robert Frost, the fishing stories of Dana Lamb are often spare and deceptively simple, using images and memories of both fishing and country things as metaphors for life itself." (*Fly Fisherman*)
". . . a fine edition that will delight any reader who enjoys a literate response to nature." (*Country Journal*)
A deluxe collector's edition of thirty-five pieces by this renowned sportsman and author.

GOOSE HUNTING by Charles Cadieux.
208 pages, 6 1/8″ × 9¼″, photographs, cloth, $14.00.

The author, a lifelong waterfowl hunter and outdoor writer, artfully interweaves lively, personal stories of goose hunting from Quebec to Mexico with an encyclopedia of facts about good management, good goose hunting and goose watching. With humor and warmth Cadieux covers the controversy about short-stopping, goose calling and its champions, decoys, the migration paths of geese, and much more.
"Anyone else thinking about writing on the subject ought to look at Cadieux's book before starting." (*Washington Post*)

THE WACKY WORLD OF SKIING by Craig Peterson, cartoons by Jerry Emerson.
128 pages, 6″ × 9″, cloth, $9.95.

Skiers don't need snow to chuckle at their favorite sport! Author Craig Peterson and cartoonist Jerry Emerson have collaborated to produce a unique book of over 100 hilarious cartoons about downhill and cross-country skiing. Emerson's cartoons have appeared in trade journals and major magazines such as the *Saturday Evening Post*, *Reader's Digest*, *Omni* and *Parade*. This original collection is sure to delight all skiers. The perfect Christmas gift!

Stone Wall Press Selected Regional Titles

EXPLORING NEW ENGLAND SHORES by John Waters.
208 pages, illustrated, cloth, $7.95.

Explains how the coastline was formed and how it changes; types of beaches and their inhabitants; the reward for the beachcomber—what to look for, where to find it, how to use it.
". . . a beachcomber's handbook. One can literally smell the salt air." (*Manchester Union Leader*)

ATLANTIC SURF FISHING, *Maine to Maryland* by Lester C. Boyd.
160 pages, illustrated, paperback, $4.95.

Basic equipment, lures, bottom rigs and bait. Covers technique and important fishing tips, seasoned with humorous stories. Zeroes in on where-to-go and how to fish in each state.

THE NORTHEASTERN OUTDOORS: *A Field Guide* by Steve Berman.
272 pages, photographs, maps, illustrations, Kivarbound, $7.95.

Practical, exciting and factual information about our natural world, complete with vivid photographs. A travel guide for more than 100 nature trips throughout the area—including maps and concise directions.

NORTHEASTERN BASS FISHING by Bob Elliot.
144 pages, illustrated, paperback, $4.95.

An updated, expanded edition that includes the "where" and "how" of bass fishing in New York, Pennsylvania, New Jersey, Delaware and Maryland—plus tips from their top bass fishermen/sportswriters.

MY NEW ENGLAND by Frank Woolner.
176 pages, illustrated, cloth, $10.00.

". . . destined to become one of the classics that will live on." (*The Massachusetts Outdoorsman*)
"While Frank's book is of New England, it is no more just for New Englanders than were the writings of Burroughs or Thoreau." (*The Blade, Toledo*)
Fifty seven short tales that follow the seasons of New England and reflect the best of this renowned outdoor writer.

STONE WALL PRESS

Bookstores, ski shops, and other retail accounts that would like to stock copies of THE WACKY WORLD OF SKIING and/or any of our other publications should contact our distributor:

Mr. Alan Hood, Sales Manager
The Stephen Greene Press
Brattleboro, VT 05301

Retail trade orders are welcomed and standard terms and discounts apply. Stephen Greene Press subscribes to the Single Title Order Plan.

Individuals wishing to order any of our books that are unavailable through a bookstore should indicate the title and number of copies desired on the coupon below and send it with check or money order (including $1.00 for postage and handling) to: The Stephen Greene Press, Brattleboro, VT 05301.

Send coupon with check or money order
(including postage) to:

The Stephen Greene Press
Brattleboro, VT 05301

Name

Address

Zip

Title   Price

Total